Number CONNECTIONS

Textbook 1

Green level

Rose Griffiths

Heinemann

Heinemann Educational Publishers
Halley Court, Jordan Hill, Oxford OX2 8EJ
a division of Reed Educational & Professional Publishing Ltd

Oxford Melbourne Auckland
Florence Prague Madrid Athens
Singapore Tokyo Sao Paulo
Chicago Portsmouth NH (USA) Mexico City
Ibadan Gaborone Johannesburg
Kampala Nairobi Kuala Lumpur

First published 1997

00 99 98 97
10 9 8 7 6 5 4 3 2 1

ISBN 0 435 53396 7
0 435 53336 3 (pack of 6)
0 435 53339 8 (1 to 3)

Designed and typeset by Susan Clarke
Illustrated by Mick Reid and Jeff Edwards
Cover design by Ron Kamen
Printed and bound in Great Britain by Scotprint

The author and publishers would like to thank teachers at the following schools for their help in trialling these materials:
Folville Junior School, Leicester
Knighton Fields Primary School, Leicester
Plymouth Grove Primary School, Manchester
Emmer Green Primary School, Reading
St John's CE (Controlled) Primary School, Sevenoaks

Contents

- Counting and place value
- Addition and subtraction
- Multiplication and division
- Mixed problems

Counting pieces

1

2 Are they all here?

How many pieces?

3

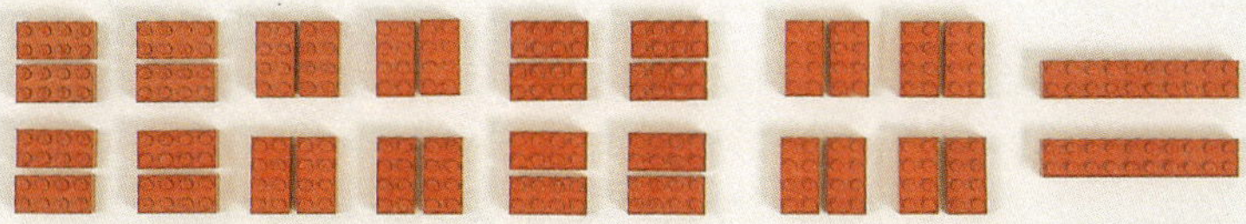

4

5

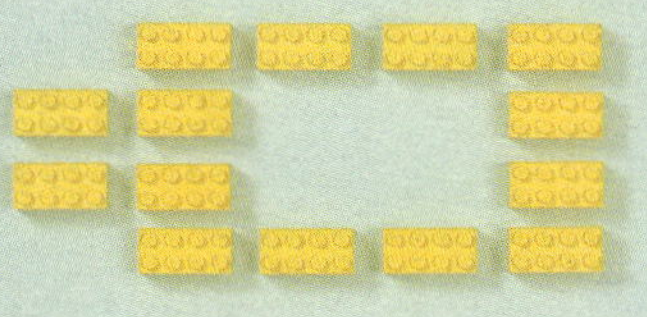

6

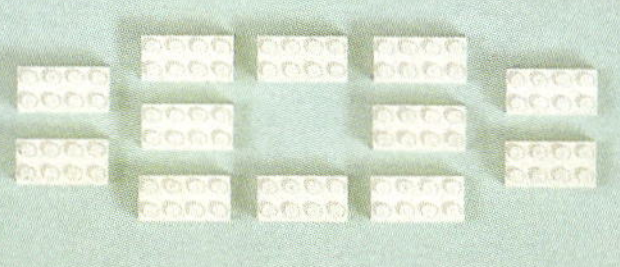

7

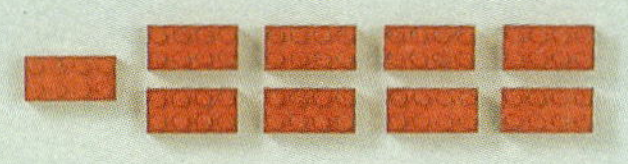

8

9 How many pieces altogether?

Spell to one hundred

50	fifty
60	sixty
70	seventy
80	eighty
90	ninety
100	hundred

Use sums to practise your spelling.

Write the answers as words.

1 Forty add ten

2 Twenty add fifty

3 Fifty add forty

4 Twenty add eighty

5 Thirty add forty

6 Thirty add thirty

7 Forty add forty

8 Ninety add ten

9 Fifty add fifty

10 Twenty add sixty

11 Thirty add sixty

12 Eighty add ten

13 Seventy add ten

14 Eighty add twenty

thirty

six

Put words together like this.

thirty six **36**

Use the word cards from the 'Ninety-nine' game.

You need word cards made from Copymaster G26.

Make each number with word cards.
Then write it down.

15 21 **16** 53 **17** 65 **18** 84

19 30 **20** 72 **21** 47 **22** 99

Ask your teacher if you can play the 'Ninety-nine' game.

► Copymasters G2 and G3
and the 'Ninety-nine' game (G24, G25 and G26)

Elevens

1 How many grapes?

Copy and complete.

2 6 + ☐ = 11

3 7 + ☐ = 11

4 8 + ☐ = 11

5 9 + ☐ = 11

6 10 + ☐ = 11

7 11 + ☐ = 11

8

I had 11 grapes.
I ate 5. How many left?

9

I had 11 cherries.
I ate 7. How many left?

10

I had 11 cherries.
I ate 3. How many left?

11

I had 11 grapes.
I ate 9. How many left?

All these sums make 10 or 11.
Copy and complete.

12 8 + 3

13 4 + 7

14 5 + 5

15 6 + 4

16 4 + 6

17 6 + 5

18 3 + 8

19 7 + 3

20 7 + 4

21 3 + 7

22 5 + 6

23 8 + 2

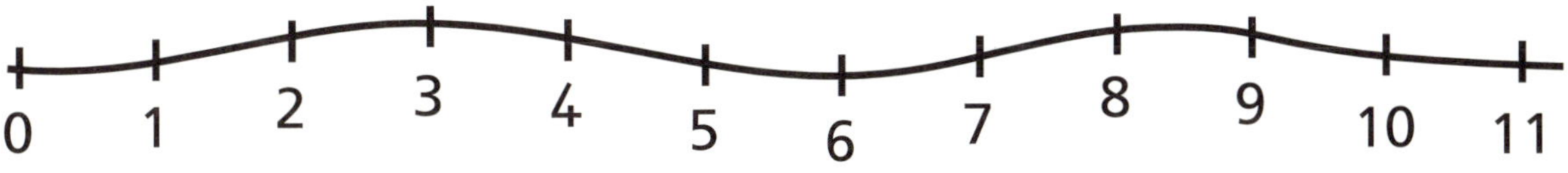

Use the number line to take away.

24 11 – 4

25 11 – 2

26 11 – 3

27 11 – 1

28 11 – 5

29 11 – 6

Ask your teacher if you can play the 'Elevens' game.

► Copymaster G4
and the 'Elevens' game (G27 and G28)

Disco

Add up these scores.

1 5 6 7

2 8 6 7

3

4 3 6 5

5 7 7 8

6

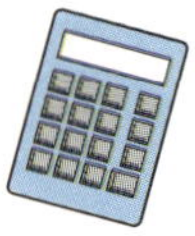 ✓ or ✗

Add up these scores.

7 5 4 6

8 10 9 10

9 7 5 8

10 5 7 5

11 What score was this?

12 What score was this?

Ten times table

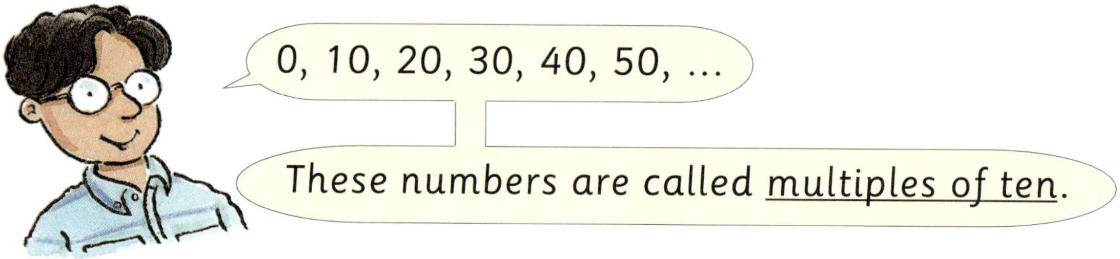

You can get multiples of ten by adding tens, or by multiplying by ten.

One £10 note

1 How much money?

2 1 × 1 0 =

Three £10 notes

3 How much money?

4 10 + 10 + 10

5 3 × 1 0 =

Five £10 notes

6 How much money?

7 10+10+10+10+10

8 5 × 1 0 =

Seven £10 notes

9 How much money?

10 10+10+10+10+10+10+10

11 7 × 1 0 =

Eight £10 notes

12 How much money?

13 10+10+10+10+10+10+10+10

14 [8] [×] [1] [0] [=]

Nine £10 notes

15 How much money?

16 10+10+10+10+10+10+10+10+10

17 [9] [×] [1] [0] [=]

18 How many £10 notes?

19 10+10+10+10+10+10+10+10+10+10

20 [1] [0] [×] [1] [0] [=]

21 Copy and complete.

Ten times table

$0 \times 10 =$	$4 \times 10 =$	$8 \times 10 =$
$1 \times 10 =$	$5 \times 10 =$	$9 \times 10 =$
$2 \times 10 =$	$6 \times 10 =$	$10 \times 10 =$
$3 \times 10 =$	$7 \times 10 =$	

Twelves

1 How many is a dozen?

2 How many chicks?

3 How many eggs left?

4 2 + 10 =

5 12 − 2 =

6 How many chicks?

7 How many eggs left?

8 4 + 8 =

9 12 − 4 =

10 How many chicks?

11 How many eggs left?

12 6 + 6 =

13 12 − 6 =

Copy and complete.

14 5 + ☐ = 12

15 6 + ☐ = 12

16 7 + ☐ = 12

17 8 + ☐ = 12

18 9 + ☐ = 12

19 10 + ☐ = 12

20 11 + ☐ = 12

21 12 + ☐ = 12

22 How much money?

23 How much money?

24

I had 12p.
I lost 2p.
How much did I have left?

25

I had 12p.
I spent 8p.
How much left?

26

I had 12p.
I spent 12p.
How much left?

Ask your teacher if you can play the 'Twelves' game.

► Copymaster G9
and the 'Twelves' game (G29 and G30)

Speedy sums

T

Work with a friend.

Write question numbers 1 to 20.
Ask your friend to read the questions to you.

Write your answers as quickly as you can.

1 3 + 5
2 9 + 2
3 0 + 7
4 3 + 3
5 7 + 5
6 4 + 6
7 1 + 4
8 12 − 9
9 8 − 2
10 9 − 7
11 10 − 1
12 10 − 5
13 4 − 2
14 11 − 8
15 7 + 3
16 12 − 2
17 6 + 6
18 9 − 1
19 5 + 4
20 5 − 5

✓ or ✗

Now you read the questions to your friend.

Do these all make 11?
Write Yes or No.

21 5 + 6

22 4 + 8

23 3 + 8

24 6 + 6

25 7 + 2

26 9 + 2

Do these all make 8?
Write Yes or No.

27 4 + 5

28 3 + 6

29 12 – 4

30 11 – 3

31 4 + 4

32 0 + 8

33 7 + 1

34 11 – 4

35 10 – 2

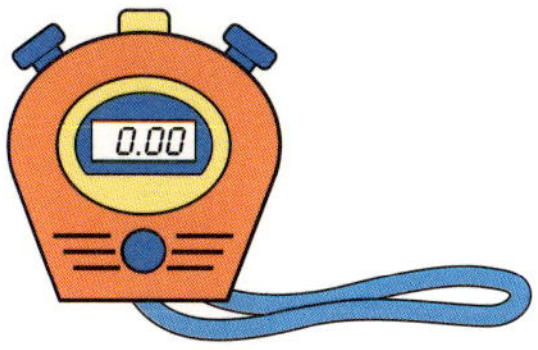

Use a stopwatch
or a sand timer.

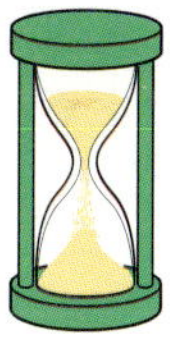

Use Speedy sums I made from Copymaster G10.

G10

Speedy sums ①
1 2 3 minute test

Name ____
Date ____

4 + 5 = ____	8 – 5 = ____	10 + 2 = ____
7 + 2 = ____	11 – 7 = ____	10 – 8 = ____
9 + 3 = ____	5 – 3 = ____	6 + 5 = ____
1 + 11 = ____	12 – 7 = ____	11 – 4 = ____
6 + 4 = ____	9 – 1 = ____	3 + 5 = ____
0 + 9 = ____	11 – 2 = ____	10 – 3 = ____
3 + 6 = ____	11 – 3 = ____	Score: ____

Can you get
20 sums right
in 3 minutes?

Check your answers. ✓ or ✗
Count how many you got right.

Talk to your teacher
about what to do next.

Twenty to forty

$$20 + 6 = 26$$

Make each number with tens and ones. Copy and complete.

Twenty-three	**1** 20 + 3 = **2** 3 + 20 =
Thirty-five	**3** 30 + 5 = **4** 5 + 30 =
Twenty-eight	**5** 20 + 8 = **6** 8 + 20 =
Thirty-one	**7** 30 + 1 = **8** 1 + 30 =
Thirty-nine	**9** 30 + 9 = **10** 9 + 30 =

✓ or ✗

Use tens and ones. Copy and complete.

11
  22
+ 6
_____

12
  14
+ 15
_____

13
  32
+ 6
_____

14
  19
+ 20
_____

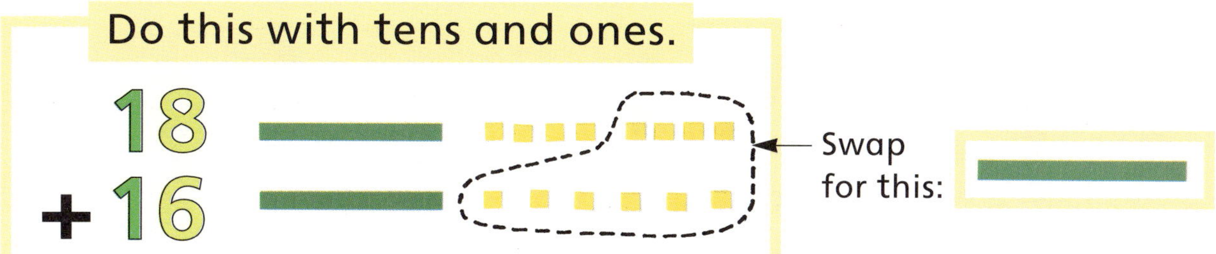

Use tens and ones. Copy and complete.

15
  30
+ 10
_____

16
  25
+ 11
_____

17
  18
+ 15
_____

18
  20
+ 17
_____

19
  17
+ 17
_____

20
  20
+ 20
_____

21
   8
+ 31
_____

22
  13
+ 19
_____

23
  15
+ 25
_____

24
  14
+ 19
_____

Half each

T

What is half of 6?

6 ÷ 2 = 3

Half of 6 is 3.

1 What is half of 4?

2 4 ÷ 2 =

3 What is half of 10?

4 1 0 ÷ 2 =

5 What is half of 14?

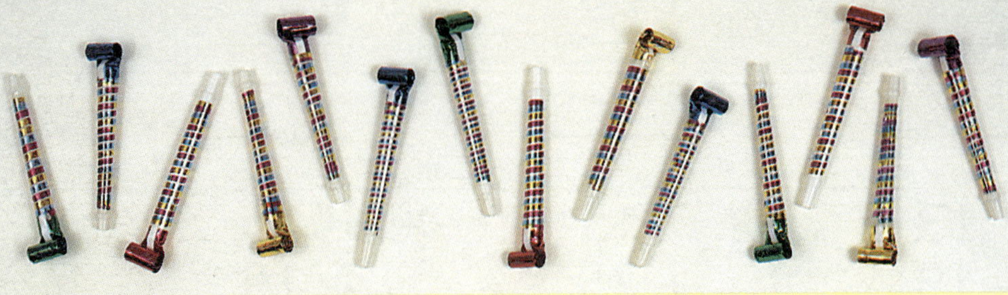

6 1 4 ÷ 2 =

7 What is half of 8?

8 8 ÷ 2 =

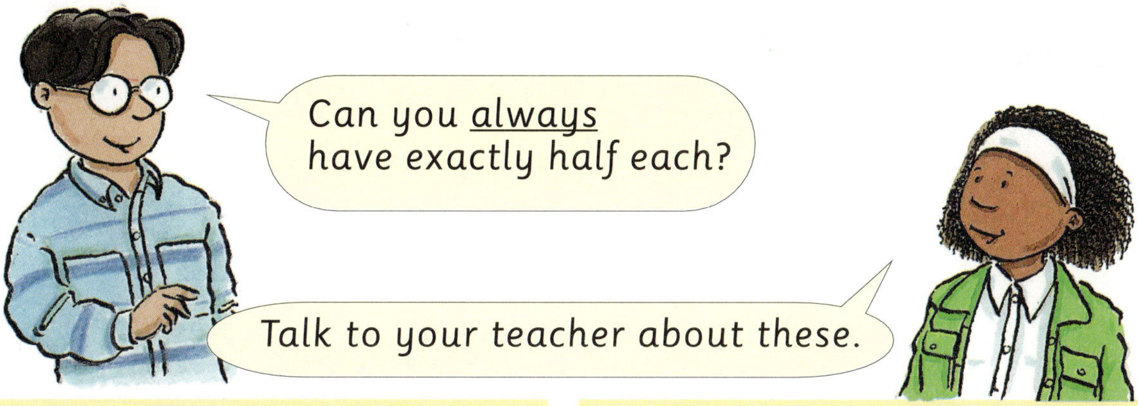

9 satsumas

9 big marbles

9

10

Tables square

Sometimes I write my times tables like this:

Sometimes I write them on a tables square:

×	0	1	2	3	4	5
0			0			0
1			2			5
2			4			10
3			6			15
4			8			20
5			10			25

When this is finished, we can use it to check tables facts up to 5 × 5.

For example, 4 × 5 = 20

Do these. Check them on the tables square.

1 3 × 2

2 2 × 5

3 5 × 5

4 2 × 2

5 3 × 5

6 0 × 5

7 4 × 2

8 1 × 2

9 The 0 times table is missing from the tables square! Copy and complete.

Nought times table

0 × 0 =

1 × 0 =

2 × 0 =

3 × 0 =

4 × 0 =

5 × 0 =

10 The 1 times table is missing from the tables square! Copy and complete.

One times table

0 × 1 =	2 × 1 =	4 × 1 =
1 × 1 =	3 × 1 =	5 × 1 =

✓ or ✗

Copy and complete.

11 2 × 4 → 2 lots of 4 → 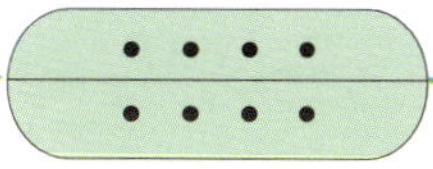 → 2 × 4 =

12 3 × 4 → 3 lots of 4 → 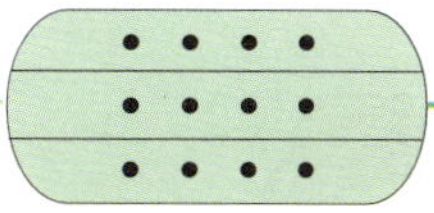 → 3 × 4 =

13 4 × 4 → 4 lots of 4 → 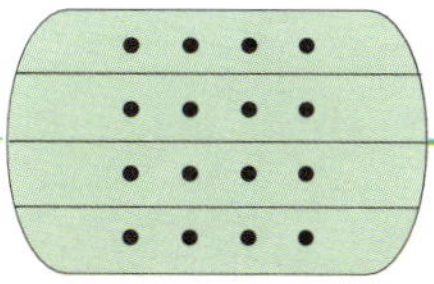 → 4 × 4 =

14 5 × 4 → ___ lots of 4 →  → 5 × 4 =

Snacks

How much will they cost?
Use coins and a calculator if you want to.

1 2 apples, please.

2 A packet of crisps and a box of raisins, please.

3 A banana and a bag of nuts, please.

4 2 packets of crisps, please.

5

3 apples, please.

6 A bag of nuts and a box of raisins, please.

7 2 bananas, please.

8 2 bags of nuts, please.

Copy and complete.

9 50 − 45 =

10 45 + ☐ = 50

50p to spend.

11 How much for these?

12 How much change?

50p to spend.

13 How much for these?

14 How much change?

50p to spend.

15 How much for these?

16 How much change?

17 If <u>you</u> had 50p, what snacks would you buy?

18 How much change would you get?

More adding

T

When I add up in my head,
I add tens first, then ones.

24 + 22 ...
that's 20 + 20 = 40,
add 4, add 2 makes <u>46</u>.

Work with a friend.
Talk to your friend about <u>how</u> you did each sum.

1 21 + 13 **2** 32 + 11 **3** 15 + 25

4 16 + 20 **5** 22 + 22 **6** 13 + 30

 ✓ or ✗.

When I add up on paper,
I add ones first, then tens ...

because sometimes I swap
ten ones for a ten.

$$\begin{array}{r} 16 \\ +\,16 \\ \hline 32 \end{array}$$

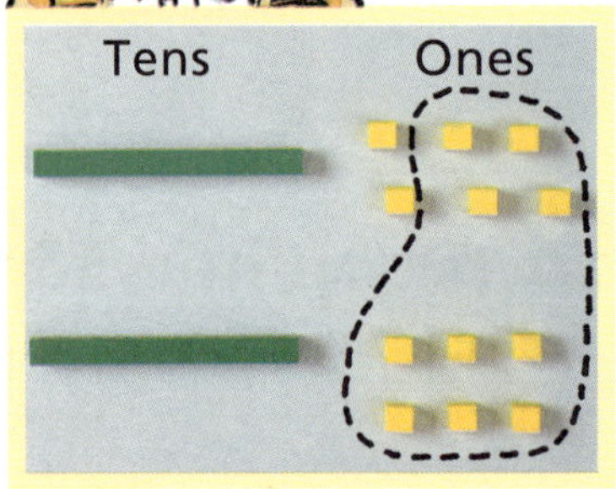

I write it like this.

6 add 6 makes 12 ...

10 add 10 add 10 makes 30.

When I added these tens, I just said '1 add 1 add 1 makes 3'.

Use tens and ones to add these. Then add up on paper.

7 $26 + 17$ = ____

8 $18 + 24$ = ____

9 $16 + 18$ = ____

10 $11 + 29$ = ____

11 $28 + 13$ = ____

12 $23 + 9$ = ____

Talk to your teacher about these sums.

► Copymasters G18 and G19

Cinema

I want to see 'Spike'.

That's Screen Two.

1  I want to see 'Ghost City'.

Which screen is it on?

2  I want to see 'Shipwreck!'.

Which screen is it on?

How much will it cost?

3 1 adult and 2 children, please.

4 3 children and 2 adults, please.

5 3 adults and 1 child, please.

6 1 adult and 4 children, please.

7 1 adult and 3 children, please.

8 2 adults and 2 children, please.

What is the next time we can see each film?

9

10

11

12

Use Copymasters G20 and G21 to run your own box office.

Marbles

What did we score?

1

2

3

4

5

6

7

How many marbles?

8

How many marbles?

9

How many marbles?

10

How many marbles?

11

How many marbles?

12

How many marbles?

Copy and complete.

13 0×4

14 1×4

15 2×4

16 3×4

17 4×4

18 5×4

19 $20 \div 4$

20 $16 \div 4$

21 $12 \div 4$

22 $8 \div 4$

23 $4 \div 4$

24 $0 \div 4$

► Copymasters G22 and G23

≈ Take two numbers ≈

T

You need a tub of number tiles.

A game for 2 people.

Take two numbers from the tub ...

and make the biggest number you can.

Then your friend does the same.

I win!

The person with the biggest number wins all 4 tiles.

Keep going until the pot is empty.